HORACE
MANN
LECTURE
1972

THE HORACE MANN LECTURESHIP

To commemorate the life of Horace Mann, 1796–1859, and in recognition of his matchless services to the American public school system, the School of Education of the University of Pittsburgh, in cooperation with the Tri-State Area School Study Council, established the Horace Mann Lectureship. The striking and varied contributions of Horace Mann must ever be kept alive and be reemphasized in each generation. It is difficult, indeed, to assess the magnitude of Mann's educational services. Turning from the profession of law, he devoted his life to the study and improvement of education. He, more than any other, can truly be called "Father of the American Public School System." His boundless energy, coupled with a brilliant and penetrating mind, focused the attention of the citizens of his era on the need for the improvement and support of public schools. His services were manifold. It shall be the purpose of these lectures to reaffirm his faith in free schools and to call to their service all citizens of this generation. It is vital that all understand the purpose and function of a free public school system in American democracy.

Full State Funding
of Education

EVOLUTION AND
IMPLICATIONS

Roe L. Johns

UNIVERSITY OF PITTSBURGH PRESS

OR 2/75

Library of Congress Catalog Card Number 72-91863
ISBN 0-8229-3258-X
Copyright © 1973, University of Pittsburgh Press
All rights reserved
Media Directions, Inc., London
Manufactured in the United States of America

The quotations from *Financing Education: Fiscal and Legal Alternatives*, edited by Roe L. Johns, Kern Alexander, and K. Forbis Jordan, are used by permission of the publisher, Charles E. Merrill Company, Columbus, Ohio.

CONTENTS

About the Author   vii

The Early History of School Financing   3

The Contributions of Theorists to
    School Financing   12

The Impact of Court Decisions on
    School Financing   31

The Findings and Recommendations
    of the National Educational Finance
    Project   41

Notes   67

ABOUT THE AUTHOR

Roe L. Johns has been Professor of Educational Administration, University of Florida, since 1946. During his years there, he has also been Financial Consultant to the National Citizens Committee for Public Schools, Executive Secretary of the Southern States Work Conference, Financial Consultant to the White House Conference on Education, and a consultant on educational finance for twenty states. He is currently Director of the National Educational Finance Project.

Dr. Johns is coauthor of *Educational Organization and Administration*, 1968, *The Economics and Financing of Education*, 1969, and *Planning School Finance Programs*, 1972. He has also coauthored or coedited the following publications of the National Educational Finance Project: volume 1, *Dimensions of Educational Need*, 1969; volume 2, *Economic*

Factors Affecting the Financing of Education, 1971; volume 3, *Planning to Finance Education,* 1971; volume 4, *Status and Impact of Educational Finance Programs,* 1971; and volume 5, *Alternative Programs for Financing Education,* 1971.

He was given the Distinguished Service Award by the American Association of School Administrators in February 1972 and was awarded an Honorary Doctoral Degree in Public Administration by the University of Florida, March 1972.

*Full State Funding
of Education*

It would require four major volumes to present a comprehensive discussion of the matters covered in the title of this essay. The titles of those volumes would be approximately as follows: (1) The Early History of School Financing, (2) The Contributions of Theorists to School Financing, (3) The Impact of Court Decisions on School Financing, and (4) The Findings and Recommendations of the National Educational Finance Project. Each of these topics will be treated in the following sections.

THE EARLY HISTORY
OF SCHOOL FINANCING

From colonial times, public schools have been financed in some of the New England states partly from taxation. In other states, however, prior to 1800 public education was considered primarily as a family or church responsibility (except for the children of paupers). Thus in all but the New England states, colonial elementary and secondary education was financed primarily from philanthropy, fees, and rate bills. Free public schools were extended very gradually during the first quarter of the nineteenth century. However, during the period from 1830 to 1860 constitutional and statutory authorization for tax-supported public schools was generally provided in the middle Atlantic and midwestern states. Legal authorization for tax-supported public schools was not generally provided in the southern states until the last quarter of the nineteenth century.

We are likely, however, to overestimate the extent of free public education available in the nation prior to the middle of the nineteenth century. According to the seventh census of the United States, in 1850 only about one-half the children in New England were provided free education, one-sixth in the West, and one-seventh in the middle Atlantic states.[1] Therefore, for many years, constitutional and statutory authorization for tax-supported public schools did not result in actual substantial tax revenues for these schools in most states. In the South, with few exceptions, free education was provided only for paupers. Even in the New England, middle Atlantic, and western states, public education was confined largely to the elementary grades and tax funds were usually supplemented by fees and rate bills. It has been a long and arduous struggle to provide free public elementary and secondary education in the United States.[2] In fact, tax-supported, free public education did not become generally available in the United States until well into the first quarter of the twentieth century. Secondary education did not become available in many rural areas until after the close of World War I.

The history of the financing of public education is a fascinating subject. A treatise on the social, economic, political, and religious history of the United States could be centered around the history of the financing of U.S. public schools. Although not specifically addressing themselves to the history of financing the public schools, many historians have revealed their sensitivity to the effect of social, economic, political, and religious factors on school financing: for example, Ellwood P. Cubberley in *Public Education in the United States,* Charles A. and Mary R. Beard in *The Rise of American Civilization,* Newton Edwards and Herman G. Richey in *The School in the American Social Order,* and Merle Curti in *The Social Ideas of American Educators.* The names of many other historians cognizant of these issues could, of course, be added to this list. Therefore, the study of the financing of public education should not be considered as an exercise in statistical analysis or a problem of data storage. *A nation's school-financing policies are a reflection of the value choices of its people, the order of priorities they establish in the allocation of their resources, and their political philosophy.*

Public education was not started in this nation from altruistic motives: in New England, for example, religious indoctrination was the primary purpose for its establishment. After the adoption of our Constitution in 1789 and continuing past the advent of the industrial revolution, public education was inaugurated primarily because it benefited business and industry, it promoted law and order, and, as suffrage was extended, it was deemed necessary for the safety of the nation under a system of popular government. Prior to the beginning of the twentieth century, public education was provided primarily to benefit and protect the adult society, not the children. The needs of adults, not the needs of children, were the principal determinants not only of whether free public education was provided but also of what was taught in the public schools and how it was taught.

Thaddeus Stevens, in his eloquent plea to the Pennsylvania House of Representatives in 1835 for the continuance of tax-supported public schools, stated the following:

> If an elective republic is to endure for any great length of time, *every* elector must have sufficient information, not only to accumulate wealth, and take care of his pecuniary concerns, but to direct wisely the legislatures, the ambassadors, and the executive of the na-

tion—for *some* part of all these things, *some* agency in approving or disapproving of them, falls to every freeman. If then, the permanency of our government depends upon such knowledge, it is the duty of government to see that the means of information be diffused to every citizen. This is a sufficient answer to those who deem education a private and not a public duty—who argue that they are willing to educate their *own* children, but not their *neighbor's* children.[3]

You will note that Thaddeus Stevens did not argue that free public education was a right of the child but rather that it was necessary to accumulate wealth and to protect the adult society. It is possible that Stevens did believe in the right of children to an education; however, he was a politician and he probably used the arguments that he believed to be effective at that time in arguing his case. It was not until well into the twentieth century, as I shall show later, that the rights of children to educational opportunity as citizens of the United States were legally recognized.

Let us now turn to the role that professional educators played in the establishment of tax-supported, free public schools. Prior to 1860 professionally trained educators provided very little leadership for the establishment of free public education. As a matter of fact, very little professional training was provided for educational leadership prior to 1900. Some schoolmasters of private schools actually opposed the establishment of free public schools. They were schooled in the European tradition of an elitist society fostered by an elitist system of education. Therefore, practically all the leadership for establishing tax-supported, free public schools was furnished by individuals from the lay public. Even Horace Mann (who became Secretary of the State Board of Education of Massachusetts in 1837) and his contemporary Henry Barnard (chief state school officer of both Rhode Island and Connecticut), both of whom had powerful influence on the establishment of tax-supported public schools, were trained as lawyers.

Even organized labor played a more important role in the establishment of free public education prior to 1860 than organized education. Organized labor had begun to gain strength in some of the middle Atlantic states by the end of the first quarter of the nineteenth century. An association of committees of workingmen in Philadelphia expressed the view of labor on education in a report adopted in 1830 as follows:

> When the committees contemplate their own condition, and that of the great mass of their fellow laborers; when they look around on the glaring inequality of society, they are constrained to believe, that, until the means of equal instruction shall be equally secured to all, liberty is but an unmeaning word, and equality an empty shadow, whose substance to be realized must first be planted by an equal education and proper training in the minds, in the habits, and in the feelings of the community.[4]

The Supreme Court of the United States in 1954 in the *Brown* v. *Board of Education of Topeka* opinion and the Supreme Court of California in the *Serrano* v. *Priest* opinion in 1971 finally expressed the same opinion. It seems strange that it took the nation a century and a quarter to accept the political and educational philosophy so clearly stated by a relatively uneducated group of Philadelphia labor leaders in 1830.

During the last quarter of the nineteenth century, tax-supported public education spread throughout the nation. The southern states, suffering from the devastation of the Civil War and resulting poverty, were the last to establish tax-supported public schools. We should not, however, assume that all children in the United States had access to elementary and secondary education by 1900. It is true that practically all children had access to some kind of elementary education, but it varied greatly in quality. In some rural sections of the nation, elementary schools were open for only three or four months each year while urban schools generally operated for eight or nine months each year. In 1900, in many rural counties, no high schools were available. It was only in the cities that both public elementary and secondary education was generally available. Therefore, educational opportunity was very unequal in the United States in 1900.

During the latter part of the nineteenth

century, educational leadership began to take an active part in the development and improvement of public education. The city superintendency of public schools was well established by 1900, and many of these men became active leaders in the development of public education. Educational associations began to influence the development of public education: both the National Education Association and the American Association of School Administrators had their roots in the nineteenth century.

THE CONTRIBUTIONS OF THEORISTS TO SCHOOL FINANCING

At the beginning of the twentieth century, professionally trained educators with a background in theory emerged as leaders in the establishment of policies for public-school financing. These men, unlike Horace Mann and Henry Barnard, did not hold public office; they were university professors and theorists. In fact, it has been observed that

all important social movements have had an
intellectual leader or leaders. These men, who
are almost always theorists, are sometimes considered impractical by the general public. However, it is the theorists who shape social policy
and social organization more than any other
group in society. Politicians and public officials
usually base their policies on theoretical as-
sumptions of some kind. Politicians such as
Jefferson, Hamilton and Madison, who were
also theorists, have had a profound effect on
governmental policy in the United States.[5]

The early theorists on school finance had
a profound influence on the political policy
of school financing in the United States.
They dealt with some of the crucial values,
issues, and problems in American society;
therefore, what they had to say was of great
interest to the public. Some of the major
questions which they attempted to answer
were: Is equalization of educational opportunity a function of a democratic government? What level of education should be
guaranteed to everyone in order to promote the general welfare? To what extent
should the states exercise control over the
public schools? To what extent should

"home rule" in school government be encouraged? Are nonproperty state taxes more equitable than local property taxes? What percentage of school revenue should be provided from state sources? Is public education a child's constitutional right?[6] In the following sections, I will discuss briefly several of the top educational theorists and their impact on public-school financing.

Ellwood P. Cubberley

The development of the theory of state school support began with Ellwood P. Cubberley, who was a student at Teachers College, at the beginning of the twentieth century. His famous monograph, *School Funds and Their Apportionment,* a revision of his doctoral dissertation, was published in 1905. It is interesting to note that George D. Strayer, Sr. (who is discussed in another section), also received his doctor's degree at Teachers College in 1905. These two were among the first professors of educational administration — Strayer stayed at Teachers College, and Cubberley went to Stanford University — and they were largely responsible for developing the early literature of educational administration and school finance. The conceptualizations of school finance developed by these two men, their students, and students of their students have dominated the thinking on educational finance during the first three-quarters of the twentieth century.

Cubberley's work was fundamental in formulating the basic concepts of state school financing. He studied the historical development of education in the United States, the legal arrangements provided for public education, the effect of the industrial revolution on the distribution of wealth, and the inequalities of educational opportunity among the several districts of a state. He then formulated his concept of the state's responsibility for providing educational services as follows:[7]

> The state owes it to itself and to its children, not only to permit of the establishment of schools, but also to require them to be established,—even more, to require that these schools, when established, shall be taught by a qualified teacher for a certain minimum period of time each year, and taught under conditions

and according to requirements which the state has from time to time seen fit to impose. While leaving the way open for all to go beyond these requirements the state must see that none fall below.[8]

He applied his basic concept of state responsibility to the apportionment of state school funds in the following words:

Theoretically all the children of the state are equally important and are entitled to have the same advantages; practically this can never be quite true. The duty of the state is to secure for all as high a minimum of good instruction as is possible, but not to reduce all to this minimum; to equalize the advantages to all as nearly as can be done with the resources at hand; to place a premium on those local efforts which will enable communities to rise above the legal minimum as far as possible; and to encourage communites to extend their educational energies to new and desirable undertakings.[9]

It is interesting to note that although Cubberley's concepts were written in 1905, they seem to be quite relevant today. Although some of us may disagree with his "reward for effort" advocacy, Cubberley was far in advance of the prevailing concepts of his day in the matter of school financing.

Cubberley used his conceptualizations of sound school fiscal policy as criteria to evaluate state school finance plans in 1905 and to make recommendations for their improvement. Following is a brief summary of his findings and recommendations:

1. Due to the unequal distribution of wealth, the demands set by the states for maintaining minimum standards cause very unequal burdens. What one community can do with ease is often an excessive burden for another.

2. The excessive burden of communities borne in large part for the common good should be equalized by the state.

3. A state school tax best equalizes the burdens.

4. Any form of state taxation for schools fails to accomplish the ends for which it was created unless a wise system of distribution is provided.

5. (Judged by Cubberley's criteria) few states (at the beginning of the twentieth

century) had as yet evolved a just and equitable plan for distributing the funds they had at hand.

6. Paid taxes, property valuation, total population, and school census were all undesirable methods of apportionment.

7. Total enrollment, enrollment for a definite period, average membership, average daily attendance, and aggregate days' attendance are successive improvements over the census basis of apportionment.

8. Any single measure for distributing state funds is defective; but if one is used, the best single measure is the number of teachers employed.

9. The best basis for distributing state funds is the combination of the teachers actually employed and aggregate days' attendance.

10. Special incentive funds should be provided to encourage communities to provide secondary education, kindergartens, manual training, evening schools, and so forth.

11. A reserve fund should be established

for the relief of those communities which have made the maximum effort allowed by law and yet are unable to meet the minimum demands made by the state.[10]

The first four of these eleven statements are just as valid in 1972 as they were in 1905. Cubberley's influence on state school fiscal policy was so great that it was not challenged until the early post–World War I period.

Harlan Updegraff

The next school-finance theorist of note following Cubberley was Harlan Updegraff, a professor of educational administration at the University of Pennsylvania. He is not as well known as some of the other theorists on school finance but his contributions are important. He made a survey of the financial support of rural schools in New York State in 1921 and in his report recommended the following:

1. The efficient participation of citizens in the responsibilities of citizenship should

be promoted by making the extent of the state's contribution dependent upon local action.

2. The state should be neither timid nor autocratic in withholding state funds because of deficiencies in local action.

3. Special grants should be provided to encourage the introduction of new features into the schools.

4. The districts should receive support in inverse proportion to their true valuation per teacher unit.

5. Efficiency in the conduct of schools should be promoted by increasing the state grant whenever the true tax rate is increased and by lowering it whenever the local tax is decreased.

6. The plan of state aid should be so framed that it will measure precisely the elements involved and will respond promptly and surely to any change in the local districts.[11]

Updegraff proposed not only criteria for evaluating systems of state support but also techniques of state support which embodied his principles and criteria. He suggested that state funds be allocated to local school districts in inverse relationship to the valuation of property per unit of educational need but in direct relationship to the local tax effort made by a district in proportion to its taxpaying ability. In other words, he proposed that districts of less wealth be apportioned more state funds per unit of need than districts of greater wealth but that any district could receive more state funds by increasing its local tax effort. Under Updegraff's formula, a poor district, if it made the same effort, could have as much total revenue available from state and local sources as a wealthy district. Therefore, Updegraff suggested that the quality of a child's education should not depend upon the wealth per unit of need of the district but upon the local tax effort made by a district in proportion to its wealth. This concept of state support was rediscovered fifty years later by John E. Coons, Professor of Law at the University of California at Berkeley, and he renamed it the "Power Equalizing Plan."[12]

George D. Strayer and Robert Haig

George D. Strayer, Sr., a school-finance theorist equal to Cubberley in his influence on school fiscal policy, agreed with both Cubberley and Updegraff in their advocacy of the fiscal equalization of educational opportunity but disagreed with them in their advocacy of state fiscal reward for local tax effort. Strayer argued that reward for effort was inconsistent with equalization of educational opportunity.

Strayer participated in the studies of the Educational Finance Inquiry Commission which were published in thirteen volumes during the early 1920s. This was the first comprehensive study of school finance made in the United States. Strayer and a colleague, Robert Haig, were responsible for the first volume of this study entitled *The Financing of Education in the State of New York*. They devoted four pages of this volume to a statement of the theoretical conceptualization of the equalization of educational opportunity, a statement which has had more impact on school fiscal policy than the remainder of all thirteen volumes of that study. Those who tend to scoff at the value of theory might well consider this phenomenon.

Strayer and Haig described the emerging concept of equalization of educational opportunity as follows:

There exists today and has existed for many years a movement which has come to be known as the "equalization of educational opportunity" or the "equalization of school support." These phrases are interpreted in various ways. In its most extreme form the interpretation is somewhat as follows: The state should insure equal educational facilities to every child within its borders at a uniform effort throughout the state in terms of the burden of taxation; the tax burden of education should throughout the state be uniform in relation to taxpaying ability, and the provision for schools should be uniform in relation to the educable population desiring education. Most of the supporters of this proposition, however, would not preclude any particular community from offering at its own expense a particularly rich and costly educational program. They would insist that there be an adequate minimum offered everywhere, the expense of which should be considered a prior claim on the state's economic resources.[13]

These theorists stated that in order to put into effect the principle of "equalization of educational opportunity" or "equalization of school support," it would be necessary: (1) to establish schools or make other arrangements sufficient to furnish the children in every locality within the state with equal educational opportunities up to some prescribed minimum; (2) to raise the funds necessary for this purpose by local or state taxation adjusted in such a manner as to bear upon the people in all localities at the same rate in relation to their taxpaying ability; and (3) to provide adequately either for the supervision and control of all the schools or for their direct administration by a state department of education.[14]

Strayer and Haig then presented the following conceptual model of state support which incorporated the principles they advocated:

1. A local school tax in support of the satisfactory minimum offering would be levied in each district at a rate which would provide the necessary funds for that purpose in the richest district.

2. The richest district then might raise all of its school money by means of the local tax, assuming that a satisfactory tax, capable of being locally administered, could be devised.

3. Every other district could be permitted to levy a local tax at the same rate and apply the proceeds toward the cost of schools.

4. However, since the rate would be uniform, this tax would be sufficient to meet the costs only in the richest district and the deficiencies would be made up by the state subventions.[15]

They presented the following arguments against the reward for local tax effort advocated by Cubberley and Updegraff:

Any formula which attempts to accomplish the double purpose of equalizing resources and rewarding effort must contain elements which are mutually inconsistent. It would appear to be more rational to seek to achieve local adherence to proper educational standards by methods which do not tend to destroy the very uniformity of effort called for by the doctrine of equality of educational opportunity.[16]

Paul Mort

Paul Mort, one of Strayer's students, developed the technology of state support which implemented the concepts of Strayer and Haig. He not only implemented their concepts but contributed some important theoretical conceptualizations of his own. Mort proposed a particularly advanced concept of what should be included in the state-assured minimum or foundation program to be equalized. Following are the elements he recommended for inclusion:

1. An educational activity found in most or all communities throughout the state is acceptable as an element of an equalization program.

2. Unusual expenditures for meeting the general requirements due to causes over which a local community has little or no control may be recognized as required by the equalization program. If they arise from causes reasonably within the control of the community, they cannot be considered as demanded by the equalization program.

3. Some communities offer more years of

schooling or a more costly type of education than is common. If it can be established that unusual conditions require any such additional offerings, they may be recognized as a part of the equalization program.[17]

Mort, in evaluating his proposals, stated: "It cannot be hoped that these will prove exhaustive as thinking in this field develops."[18] However, his statement seems as valid today as when it was written.

Mort developed a standard measure of educational need which he called the "weighted pupil"—he attempted to weight pupils in terms of factors which caused variations in pupil costs within the same district and among the districts of a state. His work was the forerunner of much present-day research on justifiable unit-cost differentials. As we approach full state funding (which we may well do during the next decade), Mort's work in this area gains significance.

Mort was much more than a theorist and researcher; he was a disseminator of his concepts. He and many of his students worked directly with state policy makers and were instrumental in getting many state legislatures to adopt state laws providing for the equalization of educational opportunity. The author of this essay was one of those students. By 1972 forty-two states had enacted legislation that apportioned a substantial part of their state funds in such a manner as to equalize at least partially the financial support of schools.

Henry C. Morrison

Henry C. Morrison, a University of Chicago professor, is sometimes overlooked by those studying the theory of state school financing.[19] He is perhaps more noted for his theories of instruction and curriculum than for his theories in school finance. However, in 1930 Morrison wrote an important book, *School Revenue*,[20] in which he made some significant contributions to the literature on school finance. He noted the great inequalities of wealth among school districts that caused great inequalities in educational opportunity. He observed that, constitutionally, education was a state function and that local school districts had failed

to provide that function efficiently or equitably. He asserted that attempts to provide
equal educational opportunities by enlarg-
ing school districts, by offering state equalization funds—such as those advocated by
Mort—or by offering state subsidies for special purposes had failed. He theorized that
those measures would continually fail to
meet educational needs and, at the same
time, to provide an equitable system of taxation to support schools. Therefore, Morrison proposed a model of state support
whereby all local school districts would be
abolished and the state itself would become
the unit both for taxation for schools and
for administration of public schools. He
suggested that the most equitable form of
tax for the state to use for the support of
schools is the income tax.

Morrison's ideas on state school finance
were not well received. At that time, great
emphasis was being given to local initiative
and local home rule. In fact, local
self-government was almost equated with
democracy itself in the political thought of
Morrison's times. The Cubberley-Upde-

graff-Strayer-Haig-Mort axis of thought was in the mainstream of American political thought and, therefore, widely accepted.

However, the defects that Morrison saw in local financing are as evident today as in his time. Furthermore, educational opportunities are far from being equalized among school districts within most states, and there is more complaint about the inequities of local property taxes for schools than ever before. It is interesting to note that in recent years Hawaii has established a state system of education with no local school districts that is similar to the model advocated by Morrison. Morrison's model for state school financing is not as far outside of the mainstream of American thought today as it was in 1930. However, as we move toward full state and federal funding, most states will likely retain local school districts with boards of education. Hawaii is a very small state, both in population and territory, and the complete Morrison model is more applicable to a small state than to a large one.

THE IMPACT
OF COURT DECISIONS
ON SCHOOL FINANCING

Let us now turn to the influence of the courts on public-school financing. Under our theory of government, the legislative branch makes the law, the executive branch administers it, and the judicial branch interprets it. However, it is not quite that simple, since the courts do not always give the same interpretation to the law with the passage of time. To some extent, the courts are the keepers of the morals and values of the people, but as morals and values change, so the courts change. The Supreme Court of the United States gave the rationale for this policy in an opinion upholding the Social Security Act in *Helvering* v. *Davis*. The court held that the decision as to whether an expenditure is for the general welfare must be made by Congress provided it is not a display of arbitrary power. The court further stated: "Nor is the concept of general welfare static. Needs that were narrow or parochial a century ago may be interwoven in our day with the well-being of the nation. What is critical or urgent changes with the times."[21]

Court decisions during the past century and a half reveal quite a change in the values of the people. As we shall see, the courts have evolved from a determination of the rights of adults to a determination of the rights of pupils.

In the nineteenth century, when most of our public school systems were established, the issue decided by the courts was whether it was legal for the legislature to levy state taxes for the public schools or to require or authorize local units of government to levy taxes for schools. It was a legalistic issue, not a humanistic issue.

The Supreme Court of the United States held in *Shaffer* v. *Carter* that "unless restrained by provisions of the Federal Constitution, the power of the state as to the mode, form and extent of taxation is unlimited, where the subjects to which it applies are within her jurisdiction."[22]

Under the Tenth Amendment to the Constitution, public education is clearly

within the jurisdiction of the states. Therefore, during the nineteenth century, the su-
perior courts of the states generally held
that it was legal for the legislature to expend state revenues for schools and also to
require or authorize local units of government to levy taxes for schools. Examples are
as follows:

1. In 1874 in the famous Kalamazoo case
in Michigan, the court ruled that it was legal
for a school district to expend tax revenue
for the support of a high school.[23]

2. In an Indiana case in 1885, *Robinson* v.
Schenck, it was ruled that it was legal for the
legislature to levy a statewide tax to aid all
of the schools of the state.[24]

3. In a Kansas case, *State* v. *Board of Com-
missioners of Elk County* in 1899, it was held
that a county can be compelled by the state
to levy a tax rate for schools.

It is interesting to note that in these cases
the courts did not seem to be concerned
with the rights of children to equal opportunities for an education, but rather
with the legality of levying taxes for schools.

Recent years have seen a radical change in court rulings concerning education. Alexander and Jordan, after making an extensive study of this matter, concluded the following:

> Recent court decisions holding state school aid formulas unconstitutional as violative of the equal protection clause of the Fourteenth Amendment represent an evolutionary step in the courts' expansion of constitutional protections of civil rights. These decisions represent a major extension of judicial precedent in the area of students' civil rights. During the past few years the constitutional rights of students have been continually expanded, placing new limitations and restrictions on the police power of the state to regulate and control education. Courts once obliquely maintained that education was a privilege bestowed upon the individual by the goodwill of the state and that it could be altered or even taken away at state discretion. Today, however, this judicial attitude has changed to the concept that the student now possesses a constitutional right to an education.[25]

Alexander and Jordan further observed:

> The equal protection clause of the Fourteenth Amendment has been the primary vehicle by

which the courts have expanded individual rights. With the desegregation cases as the basic source of precedent, the courts have recently reached the point of invoking equal protection rights as a means of forcing redistribution of state tax sources for education. The cases harbor vast legal implication, not the least of which is their impact on the traditional role of the legislature with regard to governmental finance.[26]

In making their analysis of the evolution of court cases, Alexander and Jordan noted that there have been three generations of court decisions in the twentieth century relating to school financing. Those generations are as follows:

1. *First generation cases.* In those cases, the taxpayer was the aggrieved party. He usually was contesting a tax and even sometimes opposing the equalization of educational opportunity. His motive primarily was to save himself a few dollars.

2. *Second generation cases.* In the second generation cases, the student was the aggrieved party. In these cases, it was maintained that the educational opportunity of a

student should not depend on the fiscal ability of the district in which he lived.

3. *Third generation cases.* Not only do the third generation cases raise the question of the equalization of financial resources, but they raise the additional question of the extent to which the state must go in providing equal educational opportunity.

Under the first generation cases, state equalization laws were occasionally attacked. An example is a relatively recent South Dakota case, *Dean* v. *Coddington,* in which the constitutionality of the state's foundation-program law was challenged. The plaintiff argued that the proceeds of the state tax must be uniformly distributed as well as uniformly collected. The court held that "the constitutional provisions requiring equality and uniformity relate to the levy of taxes and not to the distribution or application of the revenue derived therefrom."[27] This was the general rule usually followed by the courts in adjudicating first generation cases of this type.

The second and third generation cases

were greatly affected by the ruling of the Supreme Court of the United States in the famous *Brown* v. *Board of Education of Topeka* case. In that case the court said:

> Today, education is perhaps the most important function of state and local government. . . .
> In these days, it is doubtful that any child may reasonably be expected to succeed in life if he is denied the opportunity of an education. Such an opportunity, where the state has undertaken to provide it, is a right which must be made available to all on equal terms.[28]

Space does not permit a comprehensive discussion of the second generation cases. The most famous of these cases is a decision of the California Supreme Court in *Serrano* v. *Priest* in 1971. The court in studying whether the California system of financing education violated the equal protection clause of the Constitution found it necessary to determine whether "(1) education is a fundamental interest protected by the constitution, (2) wealth is a 'suspect classification,' and (3) the state has a 'compelling interest' in creating a system of school finance which makes a child's educa-

tion dependent on the wealth of his local
school district."[29]

In brief the court concluded that education is a fundamental interest protected by
the Constitution, that wealth is a "suspect
classification," and that the state has no
compelling interest in making a child's education dependent upon the wealth of his
local school district. The court then ruled
that the California system of school financing violated the equal protection clause of
the Fourteenth Amendment because it
made a child's education substantially dependent upon the wealth of the district in
which he lived.[30] Similar rulings were made
in the *Rodriguez* v. *San Antonio School District*
in Texas in 1971, in Minnesota in *Van
Dusartz* v. *Hatfield* in 1971, and in New Jersey in *Robinson* v. *Cahill* in 1972.

The third generation cases are particularly important because they may be in-
dicative of trends in future court decisions.
In these cases it is alleged that the educational needs of children differ, that per pupil costs of programs which are necessary to
meet these needs differ, and that education-

al opportunities cannot be equalized without recognizing these variations. Furthermore, it is argued that school districts vary in their percentage of high-cost pupils and, although a child's education should not depend on the wealth of the district in which he lives, it requires unequal expenditures per pupil in order to equalize educational opportunity. Therefore, the third generation cases require not only equalization of fiscal resources but also equalization of educational programs.

An important third generation case was *McInnis* v. *Shapiro.* The Illinois Supreme Court in 1968 held that the Illinois system of school financing was not unconstitutional because there was no "discoverable and manageable standards by which a court can determine when the Constitution is satisfied and when it is violated."[31] The "discoverable and manageable standards" referred to measures of educational need.

In a similar case, *Burruss* v. *Wilkerson,* the court held: "The courts have neither the knowledge, nor the means, nor the power to tailor the public moneys to fit the varying needs of these students throughout the state. We can only see to it that the outlays on one group are not invidiously greater or less than that of another. No such arbitrariness is manifest here."[32] The National Educational Finance Project has subsequently developed what is believed to be "manageable standards" for determining educational need.[33]

In a recent New Jersey case, *Robinson* v. *Cahill,* the court took a different view with respect to recognizing variations among the districts in educational need. It quoted with approval a New Jersey report which stated:[34]

> It is now recognized that children from lower socio-economic level homes require more educational attention if they are to progress normally through school. When the additional compensatory education is provided, it results in substantially higher costs. The weighting of the children from the lower income families compensates in part for the larger expenditure necessary to provide them with an adequate educational program so they may overcome their lack of educational background.[35]

The New Jersey court also commented that "education served too important a function to leave it also to the mood — in some cases the low aspirations — of a given school district, even those whose children attend schools in the same district."[36] This is particularly significant because it brings into question the constitutionality of the incentive-for-effort plan advocated by Updegraff and recently renamed "power equalizing" by Coons. The court held that the statutes of New Jersey providing for the financing of education violated both the state and the federal constitutions.

THE FINDINGS AND RECOMMENDATIONS OF THE NATIONAL EDUCATIONAL FINANCE PROJECT

The National Educational Finance Project was inaugurated in June 1968. This $2,000,000 project was financed largely by the United States Office of Education. Officials in the Office of Education who sponsored this project and those of us charged with the responsibility for administering it were well aware of pending court decisions and fully anticipated that present plans of financing education would be held unconstitutional. If *Serrano* v. *Priest, Rodriguez* v. *San Antonio Independent School District,* and *Robinson* v. *Cahill* are upheld by the Supreme Court, the plans of school financing in forty-nine of the fifty states will probably be found to be in violation of the Constitution. Only Hawaii, which has a complete state funding plan, will be able to meet the test.

The National Educational Finance Project made a four-year intensive study of school finance in the United States. Our findings were published in five numbered volumes and fifteen unnumbered volumes of special studies conducted by the central staff and directors of special satellite projects. These reports covered approximately four thousand pages. Thirty-eight professors, experts in school finance and economics, located in twenty universities participated in this study.

Briefly, we found that educational opportunities in all the states, except Hawaii, were unequal. In states with relatively large school districts, the variations among districts in equalized valuation of property per pupil usually ranged from five to one down to ten to one. In states with relatively small districts, the range frequently was greater than forty to one. State funds partly equalized these differences; however, even after receiving state equalizing funds, the variation among districts within a state in per pupil expenditures was frequently as great as three to one. The evidence is clear that equalization of educational opportunity is far from being achieved in the United States.

Furthermore, we found that an antiquated system of taxation which placed major reliance on the regressive property tax prevailed in most states. Neither equity for children nor equity for taxpayers was provided in state school finance plans in most states in 1971–72.

The staff of the National Educational Finance Project made a careful evaluation of each state's plan for financing schools. We then presented recommendations for improving both state and federal plans for the financing of education. But evaluations and recommendations are not primarily based on a data bank or masses of information. Judgments on the relative merits of alternative school-finance plans are based on one's values and basic beliefs. Therefore, the staff of the National Educational Finance Project presented a statement of its values and beliefs in volume 5 of the project's report entitled *Alternative Programs for Financing Education*. Following is an adaptation of that statement.[37]

Equalization of Educational Opportunity

We believe that the opportunity to obtain a public education appropriate to the individual needs of children and youth should be substantially equal. We believe that the educational opportunity of every individual should be a function of the total taxable wealth of the state and not limited primarily to the taxing ability in the local school district. Numerous studies have shown that educational opportunities vary widely within most states and that these variations are due principally to variation in wealth among the school districts of a state.

Children and youths vary widely in their educational needs. Many different types of educational programs are required to meet these needs. These programs also vary widely in per pupil cost. Furthermore, sparsity or density of population affects the unit costs of education. In order to provide substantial financial equalization of educational opportunity, necessary variations in the unit costs of education as well as variation in the wealth of districts must be taken into account in a state's financing plan.

Acceptance of the belief that substantially equal educational opportunity should be provided for all pupils requires that we support a policy of general federal aid for the public schools, since there are wide variations among the states in their financial ability to support education. It seems logical that if we support the proposition that the quality of public education provided by a state should be a function of the total taxable wealth of the state, we should also support the proposition that the total taxable wealth of the nation should be utilized to ensure that an adequate quality of public education is provided in every state. Undereducated, disadvantaged people move from state to state creating social, economic, and political problems wherever they go. Each state has a vested interest in the quality of education provided in other states. Therefore, the federal government as well as state and local governments must be concerned not only with the equalization of educational opportunity but also with the quantity and quality of public education. We believe in an economic system based on free enterprise, but that system is not really "free" without equality of educational opportunity.

Social Mobility

We believe that public education should tend to remove the barriers between caste and class and promote social mobility. That is the essence of the American dream. Every child, regardless of his race, national origin, religion, or the economic condition of his parents, should be given an equal chance in the public schools to develop his talents to the fullest in order that he may have equal access to the benefits of the American social, political, and economic system. This goal cannot be achieved under a system of financing education which promotes the segregation of pupils in schools by race, religion, or economic class. Any type of "voucher plan" or other type of plan for using public funds to support private schools which tends to segregate pupils in schools by race, by religion, or by economic class is subversive of the American dream. We recognize the right of parents to use their own resources to support private schools segregated by religion or economic or social class, but public funds should not be appropriated to serve private purposes under any guise.

Equity of Tax Structure

We believe that the public schools should be supported by an equitable tax structure. Usually, equity is considered as requiring: (1) equal treatment of equals; (2) distribution of the overall tax burden on the basis of ability to pay, as measured by income, by wealth, by consumption; (3) exclusion from tax of persons in the lowest-income groups, on the grounds that they have no taxpaying capacity; and (4) a progressive overall distribution of tax relative to income on the basis that tax capacity rises more rapidly than income. The present tax structure supporting the nation's public schools falls far short of meeting the equity test.

In 1971–72 approximately 7 percent of public-school revenue was derived from the federal government, 41 percent from state sources, and 52 percent from local sources. Approximately 98 percent of all tax revenue raised by local districts is derived from local property taxes. The property tax is the most regressive of any of the major types of taxes. Federal and state nonproperty taxes are more equitable than local property taxes. Therefore, the goal of improving the tax structure for the public schools must be attained primarily by increasing the percentage of revenue provided from state and federal sources.

Control of Education

We believe that decisions concerning education should be made by the lowest level of government that can efficiently make that decision. By that we mean that a decision should not be made by the federal government if it can efficiently be made by the states and a decision should not be made by the state if it can efficiently be made by local school districts. Each higher level of government should impose its power on the lower one only to establish general policies for the common good, but not to destroy that diversity which enriches without harming others.

Unfortunately, the federal government and a number of the states have occasionally enacted financial legislation incorporating central controls which prevent the most efficient use of the funds appropriated. There is no logical reason why the level of government which levies the taxes and appropriates the funds must make all of the decisions concerning their use. The presumption is that the taxes were levied and the funds appropriated to obtain desired educational outputs rather than to create central bureaucracies to exercise power that could more efficiently be exercised at lower levels of government.

District Organization

We do not believe that school district lines should be gerrymandered so as to segregate pupils by wealth, race, social or economic class. Constitutionally, education is a state responsibility, and, therefore, the states should not permit the establishment and continuation of school districts for the local governance of education which were deliberately created, or are being deliberately perpetuated, for the purpose of segregating pupils by race, wealth, and social or economic class. There is abundant evidence that many such districts exist in the United States. The goal of equalization of educational opportunity cannot be attained in states that maintain a discriminatory district organization.

Federalism

We believe in the concept of federalism as applied to education. We believe that the

ly 30 percent of school revenue, the local districts no more than 10 percent, and the states the remainder. If the United States Supreme Court upholds recent state and federal district court rulings, forty-nine of the fifty states will have to radically revise their systems of school financing in order to equalize educational opportunity. If we accept the values stated by the National Educational Finance Project, and I believe that a majority of the people of this nation believe in those values, we should equalize educational opportunity regardless of whether the courts compel us to do so. The critical issue will then be: "Will a state equalize upward or will it equalize downward?" No state or nation makes progress by reducing its advances in order to fill in low places. The best public schools we have in each state are not too good for the children who live in the districts with our poorest schools. It would be self-defeating to level our best schools down to the average and raise our poorest schools up to the average because we would end in a dead level of mediocrity. I do not think our legislatures will do this. I believe that our legislatures generally will raise educational opportunity in all districts upward to the quality level now being enjoyed by the children in the districts with the better educational programs. This will require a great deal of additional money, and a major increase in both federal and state funds will be required in order to meet this need.

Only a system of complete state and federal funding, or largely state and federal funding, of the public schools can meet the needs of the times. A satisfactory system of complete state and federal funding could be devised under which the state of average wealth would receive 30 percent of its revenue from federal sources and 70 percent from state sources, the states of less than average wealth would receive more than 30 percent from federal sources and would provide the remainder from state sources, and the states of greater than average wealth would receive less than 30 percent of their revenue from federal sources and would provide the remainder from state sources. Such a system, in order to be equitable, would, of course, have to include adjustments due to variations in costs of living, variations in cost due to sparsity of population, and variations in costs due to differences in the concentration of high-cost children. There seems to be no reason why the federal share might not be increased to more than the suggested 30 percent if conditions warrant it.

The National Educational Finance Project has proposed a plan which is a slight variation from the complete state and federal funding plan. Under this plan the federal government would provide approximately 30 percent of school revenue, local school districts no more than 10 percent, and the state the remainder. If the courts require complete financial equalization, this plan may not meet the requirements of the equal protection clause of the Fourteenth Amendment. However, the Project staff feels that a little local tax leeway is needed in order to provide for innovation and experimentation and to provide for contingencies. We would not, however, wish to return to the "lighthouse" concept which has been used to justify an elitist school system for pupils living in districts of great wealth. We believe that the benefits of the "lighthouse school system" have been greatly exaggerated. The lighthouse school system, instead of developing educational ideas which would benefit all systems regardless of wealth, has usually demonstrated only what any well-administered school system could do if it had the money.

Some fear has been expressed recently that financing schools from federal and state funds will result in a loss of local control. Actually, effective local control is a myth in a poverty-stricken school system. Increases in federal and state revenues widen the decision areas of local boards of education. An example of this is Title I of the Elementary and Secondary Education Act of 1965, which provided substantial funds for the compensatory education of the culturally disadvantaged. Prior to that time boards of education could spend but little money for this purpose, because very few state aid programs recognized this need and it was difficult to get local school revenues for this purpose. Federal aid can be provided with no objectionable controls or it can be provided with objectionable controls. The same is true of state funds. I have confidence in our representative form of government, and I believe that over the years neither Congress nor state legislatures will destroy the local control of education which provides diversity that enriches without harming others. Efficiently organized school districts can and should be continued under full state and federal funding with the same powers for the administration and supervision of the public schools that they now generally possess.

The legislature of every state must make the following major policy decisions with respect to financing the public schools:

1. What educational programs and services will be funded in the state's school-finance plan and for whom will these programs be provided?

2. Will state funds be apportioned on the flat-grant basis which ignores differences in the wealth of local school districts or on the

equalization basis which provides more state funds per unit of educational need to districts of less wealth than to districts of greater wealth?

3. Will necessary variations in unit costs of different educational programs and services be recognized or ignored in allocating state funds on either the flat-grant or equalization basis?

4. What proportion of school revenue will be provided by the state and what proportion from local sources?

5. How progressive (or regressive) will be the state's tax structure?

6. To what extent will the state provide for financial equalization of educational opportunity among school districts of the state?

7. As the state moves toward the equalization of educational opportunity, will it "level up" or "level down"?

8. What are the financial needs of the public schools and how nearly can those needs be met, taking into consideration needs for other governmental services and the financial ability of the state?[41]

State legislatures have many alternatives open to them as they face these policy issues. What is the best plan for financing education? That depends on the values and beliefs of the decision makers. Following are some options suggested by the National Educational Finance Project.

1. If one believes that educational opportunities should be substantially equalized financially among the districts of a state, but that districts should be left with some local tax leeway for enrichment of the foundation program, he will decide that an equalization model is the best model. However, the higher the priority that one gives to equalization, then the more he will prefer the equalization model that provides the most equalization.

2. If one believes that educational opportunities should be completely equalized financially among the districts of a state, he will prefer the complete state-support model. If the *Serrano* v. *Priest* decision of the Supreme Court of California in August 1971 is upheld by the United States Su-

preme Court, complete state and federal support of the public schools or complete equalization of local ability by an equalization model may be the only legal alternatives.

3. If one believes that all children regardless of differences in ability, talent, health, physical condition, cultural background, or other conditions which cause variations in educational needs have a right to the kind of education that meets their individual needs, he will select school-finance models which incorporate the programs needed and which provide for necessary cost differentials per unit of need.

4. If one believes that educational opportunity should be substantially equalized among the states, he will support a revenue model which provides a substantial percentage of school revenue in general federal aid apportioned in such a manner as to tend to equalize educational opportunities among the states.

5. If one believes that the taxes for the support of the public schools should be relatively progressive rather than regres-

sive, he will prefer revenue models which provide a high percentage of school revenue from federal and state sources.

6. If one believes that publicly financed education should tend to remove the barriers between caste and class, and provide social mobility, he will oppose any plan of school financing which promotes the segregation of pupils by wealth, race, religion, or social class.

7. If one believes that all essential functions of state and local government should be equitably financed in relation to each other, he will oppose any finance model for any function of government, including education, under which either federal or state funds are allocated to local governments on the basis of "the more you spend locally, the more you get from the central government" rather than on the basis of need.

8. If one believes that the educational output per dollar of investment in education should be maximized, he will support finance models that will promote efficient district organization and efficient organization of school centers within districts.

9. If one believes in a federal system of government, he will support finance models which will not require a decision governing public education to be made at the federal level when it can be made efficiently at the state level, and will not require a decision to be made at the state level when it can be made efficiently at the local level, regardless of the percentage of revenue provided by each level of government.

10. If one believes that education is essential to the successful operation of a democratic form of government in a free enterprise society and if he believes that education is essential to the economic growth of the nation and to the fulfillment of the legitimate aspirations of all persons in our society, he will support revenue models sufficiently financed to meet educational needs adequately.[42]

In conclusion, the struggle for freedom and equality has been as long as the history of civilization. Will we have an elitist society dominated by the privileged few, or will we have an equalitarian society where every human being has an equal chance for "life, liberty, and the pursuit of happiness"? Will we have an elitist public-school system promoting an elitist society or will we have an equalitarian school system promoting an equalitarian society? Equality is a necessary condition precedent to freedom. There can be no freedom without equality. Equality of educational opportunity, equality of protection under the law, equality of economic opportunity, and equality in receiving the benefits of constitutional rights are all conditions necessary for freedom. Let us press on toward realizing the American dream of an equal chance in life and liberty and justice for all by equalizing educational opportunity throughout this land.

NOTES

1. Newton Edwards and Herman G. Richey, *The School in the American Social Order* (Boston: Houghton Mifflin Company, 1963), p. 292.

2. Ibid., see chap. 9.

3. Hazards Register of Pennsylvania, vol. 15, no. 18, May 2, 1835.

4. Quoted by Edwards and Richey, *The School in the American Social Order*, p. 281.

5. Roe L. Johns, "State Financing of Elementary and Secondary Education," in *Education in the States: Nationwide Development Since 1900*, ed. Edgar Fuller and Jim B. Pearson (Washington, D.C.: National Education Association, 1969), p. 182. Note: The portion of this paper dealing with the theorists on school finance is either adapted from or quoted from this same source.

6. Ibid., adapted, p. 182.

7. Ibid., adapted, p. 183.

8. Ellwood P. Cubberley, *School Funds and Their Apportionment* (New York: Teachers College, Columbia University, 1905), p. 16.

9. Ibid., p. 17.

10. Ibid., adapted from pp. 250-54.

11. Harlan Updegraff, *Rural School Survey of New York State: Financial Support* (Ithaca: n.p., 1922), pp. 117-18.

12. See John E. Coons, William H. Clune, III, and Stephen D. Sugarman, *Private Wealth and Public Education* (Cambridge, Mass.: Belknap Press of Harvard University, 1970), chap. 6.

13. George D. Strayer and Robert Murray Haig, *The Financing of Education in the State of New York*, Report of the Educational

67

Finance Inquiry Commission, vol. 1 (New York: Macmillan, 1923), p. 173.

14. Ibid., p. 174.

15. Ibid., pp. 174–75.

16. Ibid., p. 175.

17. Paul R. Mort, *The Measurement of Educational Need* (New York: Teachers College, Columbia University, 1924), pp. 6–7.

18. Ibid., p. 7.

19. This section on Morrison is adapted from Johns, "State Financing of Elementary and Secondary Education," p. 192.

20. Henry C. Morrison, *School Revenue* (Chicago: University of Chicago Press, 1930).

21. Helvering v. Davis, 301 Cr. 5619, 57 Sup. Ct. 904 (1937).

22. Shaffer v. Carter, 252 U.S. 37, 40 S. Ct. 221, 64 L. Ed. 445.

23. Stuart v. School District No. 1 of Village of Kalamazoo, 30 Mich. 69 (1874).

24. Robinson v. Schenck, 1 N.E. 698, Ind. 1885.

25. Kern Alexander and K. Forbis Jordan, "Constitutional Alternatives for State School Finance," in *Financing Education — Fiscal and Legal Alternatives,* ed. Roe L. Johns, Kern Alexander, and K. Forbis Jordan (Columbus: Charles Merrill Company, Inc., 1972), p. 470.

26. Ibid., p. 471.

27. Dean v. Coddington, 81 S.D. 140, 13 N.W. 3nd 700 (1964).

28. Brown v. Topeka Board of Education, 347 U.S. 483 (1954).

29. Alexander and Jordan, "Constitutional Alternatives."

30. Summarized from Serrano v. Priest, 5 Cal. 3d 584, 487 P. 2d 1241 (1971).

31. McInnis v. Shapiro, 293 F. Supp. 327 (N.D. Ill. 1 E.D. Nov. 15, 1968).

32. Burruss v. Wilkerson, 310 F. Supp. 572 (May 23, 1969).

33. See Roe L. Johns, Kern Alexander, and K. Forbis Jordan, eds., *Planning to Finance Education* (Gainesville, Fla.: National Educational Finance Project, 1971), vol. 3.

34. Alexander and Jordan, "Constitutional Alternatives."

35. Burruss v. Wilkerson, 310 F. Supp. 572 (May 23, 1969).

36. Ibid.

37. Quoted or adapted from Roe L. Johns, Director, and Kern Alexander, Associate Director, *Alternative Programs for Financing Education*, vol. 5 (Gainesville, Fla.: National Educational Finance Project, 1971), pp. 1-7.

38. See National Educational Finance Project, *Future Directions for School Financing* (Gainesville, Fla.: The Project, 1971).

39. Brown v. Topeka Board of Education, 347 U.S. 483 (1954).

40. See Johns and Alexander, *Alternative Programs for Financing Education*, chaps. 8, 9, and 10.

41. Ibid., quoted or adapted, pp. 269-70.

42. Ibid., quoted or adapted, pp. 348-49.

THE HORACE MANN LECTURE SERIES

1953   PUBLIC EDUCATION AND A PRODUCTIVE SOCIETY
Maurice J. Thomas

1954   THE SCHOOL THAT BUILT A NATION
Joy Elmer Morgan   (out of print)

1955   THE EDUCATION OF FREE MEN
Ernest O. Melby   (out of print)

1956   EDUCATION FACES NEW DEMANDS
Francis S. Chase

1957   FISCAL READINESS FOR THE STRESS OF CHANGE
Paul R. Mort   (out of print)

1958   FACTORS THAT INFLUENCE LEARNING
Daniel A. Prescott   (out of print)

1959   THE DISCIPLINE OF EDUCATION AND AMERICA'S FUTURE
Lawrence D. Haskew   (out of print)

1960   PSYCHOLOGY OF THE CHILD IN THE MIDDLE CLASS
Allison Davis

1961   PERSONNEL POLICIES FOR PUBLIC EDUCATION
Francis Keppel

1962   EDUCATION AND THE FOUNDATIONS OF HUMAN FREEDOM
George S. Counts

1963   A DESIGN FOR TEACHER EDUCATION
Paul H. Masoner

1964   CRITICAL ISSUES IN AMERICAN PUBLIC EDUCATION
John K. Norton

1965　THE GENIUS OF AMERICAN EDUCATION
Lawrence A. Cremin

1966　SOCIAL PROBLEMS IN PUBLIC SCHOOL ADMINISTRATION
Benjamin C. Willis

1967　THE TEACHER AND THE MACHINE
Philip W. Jackson

1967　SUPPLEMENT
PRESIDENTIAL STATEMENTS ON EDUCATION
Maurice J. Thomas

1968　THE NEW CULT OF EFFICIENCY AND EDUCATION
H. Thomas James

1969　UPROOTED CHILDREN: THE EARLY LIFE OF MIGRANT FARM
WORKERS
Robert Coles

1970　EDUCATING THE DISADVANTAGED OR EDUCATING HUMAN
BEINGS?
Kenneth Clark　　　　　　　　(unpublished)

1971　HIGHER EDUCATION AND THE PACE OF CHANGE
Katherine Elizabeth McBride

1972　FULL STATE FUNDING OF EDUCATION: EVOLUTION AND
IMPLICATIONS
Roe L. Johns